Beans & Taters

Uncovering the Past

by

TONYA AVERY HINTON

DORRANCE PUBLISHING CO
EST. 1920
PITTSBURGH, PENNSYLVANIA 15238

Dorrance Publishing Co
585 Alpha Drive
Pittsburgh, PA 15238
Visit our website at *www.dorrancebookstore.com*

ISBN: 978-1-6386-7340-8
eISBN: 978-1-6386-7367-5

Beans & Taters
Uncovering the Past

Forward

So… Beans & Taters? Well, that was a term my dad used a lot when I was growing up. 'We came from beans and taters', he would say. Picture a young girl with a very confused look on her face and that was me. My dad said a lot of things I didn't understand until I was much older. *A lot of those things I can't repeat.* He was quite a character, really. But, anyway… basically he came from meager beginnings, poverty.

A few years before my mom would turn 50, I decided to look into her family tree. *I didn't know how long it may take.* She had expressed an interest in wanting to dig into it and find out where her ancestors were from. She had said that she didn't know much beyond her mom and dad's parent's names. She hadn't talked much about how she had grown up, just that she had a pretty big family (8 siblings) and loving parents. I had met all of her siblings and my grandparents and loved them all dearly. I had a very good relationship with all of them. But none of them had ever talked to me about how poor they had been… It didn't take me long to find out that my mom had come from beans and taters too. And that was the defining moment in my future… the decision to journey into my family's past changed my life, my outlook on love, my feelings about family and my feelings about true happiness. The real stuff, you know, JOY!

Chapter 1

And so it begins. I was home schooling my daughter, Felecia, and didn't work outside of our home, so I decided to incorporate doing family research into her curriculum and make it a school project as well. We loaded up book bags with paper and pencils and highlighters and a lot of other useless items and we were off to the local public library. *Have you ever noticed that the smell of the library, the smell of all those books can be intoxicating? Well, for those of us who love books anyway!* We asked at the front desk and she said we needed the Ancestry Room and that was in the basement. We jumped onto the elevator and I want to say we walked out into a magical place… But, no, it was dark and scary in that hallway and Felecia was actually about to break my hand. I was afraid, too, but I never said so. There were a couple of doors that were shut, and at the end of the hall was a plaque over a door that said "REFERENCE"; that is not what the lady at the desk had called it. But most of the door was glass and lights were on so…. Moving away from the darkness, that is where we went. Then, we walked into the magical place. A room full of smiling faces and people willing to answer all of our questions! *I did not know how much I would care for those people at the time, but many of them became good friends of mine and that was more than 15 years ago. I would love to call them by name, but that is not how the editors let you do things, so boo to them!*

I must have looked either overwhelmed or flabbergasted because a little old lady came up and said "Well, what are you wanting to get into today?" *I fell in love with her immediately. She has passed since, but she carries a special place in my heart.* I smiled my huge Avery smile, and said "I am wanting to do my mom's family tree!" I must have sounded extremely enthusiastic because she giggled at me, which made her chin hairs glisten in the light, and she handed me a tree chart and said to fill it out, as much as I knew, and then let her know when I was done. Over the course of the next few hours, I learned a million things… Ever heard of the Soundex? Me either. Or that they only release the Census information 72 years after the year it was taken to allow persons to be dead or so old, they don't care what you think about them or their business anymore. *Ha, I still think that is hilarious.* She said lots of people don't want anyone to know about the skeletons in their closets until they are dead and gone. She had me hook, line and sinker! *To this day I work a full-time job and all I think about is genealogy. On my breaks and my lunch, at home and with my friends. It defines who I am to my core, and all I want is to share my love of it with others so they can relish in their past as well.* Back to topic. I got a few generations back that day and all I wanted to do was tell my mom. But that would spoil the surprise, so I had to wait three long years. *Torture!*

In the next several months we went to the library as much as possible, digging and searching. I was learning so much, not just about my family and where they had lived and came from, but about research in general. I might stumble on something in an old newspaper that had a name that matched an ancestor and even the same town… but I would dig further. I had to be positive, if nothing else, I wanted people to know that if I put it down it was the real deal. Which is pretty much how I do everything. I am a no shades of gray kind of person; all in or not at all. Sometimes the information would be about my people and sometimes it wasn't. Didn't bother me either way, because it was the truth and that was what I was looking for. I wanted my mom to be proud of the work I had done when I finally gave it to her and to be able to say I knew for a fact that the info was accurate.

Brick wall. I had hit a wall; I had heard the other regulars say that they were at the 'Wall'. "Happens to everyone" they would say. "You will find yours too at some point". Well considering I wasn't a pro, like I felt they were, I thought what now… "Sounds like a road trip!" My little old lady friend told me. Road trip? I rejoiced at the thought. Both of my parents had originated from Muhlenberg County, KY, and that was just a 45-minute jaunt down a main highway from my hometown. So off we went, armed only with my current research and a pencil, because by now I had realized how useless all that other stuff had been, we were headed to the county seat of Muhlenberg, Greenville KY. "They have a genealogy annex across from the courthouse on Main Street", I had been told. And there it was, my heart was racing with anticipation. We walked in and Felecia said, "WOW!" It was lovely, very old and quaint looking. Thousands of books lined the oak bookshelves… doesn't get much better than this, I thought. And I was right, because the lady who walked up to me and was smiling from ear to ear spoke, SCREEEECCCHHHHH! (Record scratch) the loudest, high-pitched voice I had ever heard.

"I AM JUST HELPIN' OUT UNTIL SHE GETS BACK FROM AN ERRAND, SHOULDN'T BE 5 MINUTES MORE, BUT I CAN PROLLY POINT YOU IN THE RIGHT DIREC-TION." Wow! I thought to myself.

"Well, I was told I could probably find some information on my mother's family, they were from here. The last name is Dukes.

"WELL, (sounded like wheel) WE ARE PROLLY RE-LATED THEN! AIN'T TOO MANY FOLKS AROUND HERE THAT DON'T HAVE A DUKES IN THEIR FAMILY SOME-WHERE OR NOTHER. WE HAVE SOME FAMILY FILES IN THIS CABINET OVER HERE." She pulled out the top drawer and I immediately saw the name, she grabbed the file, laid it on the table behind us and said,

"MAKE YOURSELF AT HOME AND IF YOU NEED ANYTHING, GIVE A SHOUT." She walked over to another table and sat down in front of a book and began reading again.

I know it sounds like I am making fun of her, but I want you to know exactly what it was like. Truth be told, she may not have heard

well and that is why she was so loud. But she was very kind, and genuine. Not something that I was used to, being from a much larger city. Back to topic, I opened the file…. And tons of information was before my eyes! We were so excited! Trees that other people had completed, with a Dukes on one side or the other of their family, were in there. Obituaries, newspaper articles, copies of old photos and a copy of a page from a book. "Murderers from Muhlenberg" was the title. What was this about? My arm hairs were standing on end. "What is it, Mom?" Felecia asked me. All I could say was, "This." She came around the table and said, "Whoa!" Two different articles on the page had a Dukes name underlined… Surely, these were not my people. So, we dug in, who are the people who were murdered and why? Well, the first article was very short and to the point, Dukes shot his wife for cheating on him. And yes, he was related, but very distantly. But the second article, the killer was a lot closer relation, as were the deceased. He was my mom's cousin and he had killed his father and stepmother. Handwritten on this copy, below the article, said 'see newspaper articles in file'. And there he was, Leslie Dukes, he looked like my Papaw. Probably because his father, Henry, was my Papaw's brother… I was floored. The front page of the Greenville Leader in huge, bold letters read, "NO MOTIVE, 'I JUST WANTED TO'".

Chapter 2

"Mom"! Felecia said, "She's talking to you."

"I'm sorry?"

"I JUST SAID, HOPE YOU FIND WHAT YOU'RE LOOKING FOR." Screechy lady said with a big smile as she was heading out the door.

"Thanks so much for your help."

"Are you ok? You kinda spaced out for a sec." Felecia asked.

"I just don't know what to think about this."

"What is it, I mean I can read, but what exactly is the newspaper thing about?" she wanted to know.

"Well, this is Mamaw's cousin", I said pointing at the picture of Leslie, "And he killed his dad, Henry, who was Mamaw's Dad's brother". I was now pointing to my Papaw on our family tree chart. He died when I was little, so she never knew him.

"He killed his own Daddy"?

"That's how it looks... I need to read all of this and see what I can figure out. Let's set you up with some of these tree charts from the file and some books from the census shelf and you can help me tear down this brick wall. Ok?"

"Sure!" she said.

The lady that actually worked there had come in and I wanted to pick her brain. I pulled the newspaper article closer to my face and sat back, giving it my full attention. The stepmom had been shot in the head in bed and his dad was on the floor at the foot of the bed shot multiple times in the chest. It turned out that there were several articles that had been printed over the course of two weeks. But, they all said the same thing... no motive. In my brain, people do not just decide to kill someone. There would have to be some deep rooted something or other, *I mean come on! Right?* I was going to have to get to the bottom of this or lose my mind… I told Felecia I was going to talk to the lady. I walked toward her little desk in the center of the room, and she saw me coming.

"Hey! You finding what you're looking for?"

"A little more than I bargained for actually". "Do you know anything about the Dukes families from around here?"

"Well, I ought to, I am one!" she giggled. I liked her voice; it didn't make me want to flee from her presence.

"Well, I am just in shock over the article about Henry Dukes and his family!". She was nodding her head before I even finished the sentence.

"It really took this community by surprise. He had been in good standing in this area for years. He was in is 50's for goodness sake…" She was shaking her head sadly. "What is your connection with the Dukes?" She asked.

"My mom was a Dukes, Henry was actually her first cousin. But we have never heard anything about this. My Papaw has been gone for a long time, so I guess there was no one thinking to pick up the phone and call us. How are you a Dukes?" She got up and walked over to the table we had been sitting at and asked Felecia if she could have one of the tree charts she had been looking at.

"This is me." She pointed at the first person on the chart."This is my, I mean our, family." She was really smiling now. Obviously proud of our family and our heritage.

"Awesome, guess I am gonna be related to just about everyone here." I surmised.

"Yep", she said. "Inevitable!"

"So, what's the deal with the 'no motive' thing?" I posed the question to her, "Ever try to dig into that at all?"

"Well, I never gave it much thought", she looked confused.

"There has to be more to it than what he told the police… there was a reason." I told her, "People don't just up and decide to kill their parents." I was looking at the article in my hand again. "I am gonna have to look a little deeper just to satisfy my curiosity."

"Well, I would be very interested to know if you find any-thing. But, as for today, can I help you with anything else here at the Annex?"

"I can't find my grandfather in the 1920 Census. My mom told me his parent's names, and apparently his mom died very young, but I found his dad and my Papaw was only 8 and isn't with him." I pulled the copy of the 1920 Census out of my papers and handed it to her.

"I know these people from my research", she replied as she was walking toward the Census books on a row of shelves. She grabbed the 1920 Muhlenberg off the shelf and started flipping through it.

"Here it is… he was living with his aunt and her family. If I remember the stories correctly, his dad went to work with the railroad to make more money and his sister took in your grandfather because his mom had died." I was standing there with my mouth hanging open. *She actually knew my family... this was amazing!*

"Thank you so much, I have been looking and digging for months to try and fill in this gap!" I exclaimed. She was smiling at me, proud to help me, I'm sure. And I was overjoyed!

"Can I look through your research and see if you have any-thing I don't have", she asked me. "Sure, that would be great. You can make sure I am on the right track." So, we walked toward the table and she stopped in front of the copier to make a copy from the 1920 census. She handed it to me and said, "On the house", and then we both laughed. She was funny and I liked her. We sat down and she started looking through my papers. She was just glancing at one after the other and then she stopped and exclaimed,

"No way! I have been looking for this marriage record for ages!" I looked over her shoulder and it was my grandparent's marriage certificate.

"Yep, I looked for that for a long time myself. And actually, found it by accident. I never would have thought to look in Indiana, but I was looking for something for a friend when I stumbled onto it. Then I noticed that their ages were wrong and asked the clerk at the Spencer County courthouse what she thought about it. That's when she told me that you didn't have to prove your age there, at that time, you just showed up and got married." She was studying it thoroughly, and then she said,

"So you think they lied about their age and that's why they had to run off to get married?"

"Yep, they were actually 18 and 14, not 21 and 18… I remember my Papaw telling me one time that he remembered my Grandma playing with baby dolls when he would be leaving for work in the mornings." Now she was the one with her mouth hanging open…

"That is so neat!" she exclaimed. "Do you mind if I quote you in my wrings for my kids?" "Sure!" I said, happy to be the one with the information this time. But I was still extremely curious about the reason for those murders…

"I am really wanting to find out more about Leslie and the murders, but I don't know where to start."

"Hmmm, well…" she said, "You might get more into the marriage between his dad and step-mom and see where that gets you."

"That's good and I think I will check and see if Leslie was ever in any other trouble before."

Chapter 3

"Well, that turned up nothing," I groaned. Exhausted from my relentless searching of old newspapers and having forgotten that Leslie had spent most of his adult life in California, I had little to nothing to show for my efforts.

"Don't give up, mom," Felecia said, "we will find it!" I just smiled at her and her positive attitude. We were back at our local library, and after several weeks and attempts, were still at it. "This is weird," she said.

"What?"

"Remember when we went to the cemetery in Greenville, I think, right?" She was puzzled… "And we took all those pictures of the gravestones?"

"Yes, that was Greenville. What's weird? What'cha lookin' at?"

"The step-mom has the same death date as this lady in the picture. You had said she was buried with her dad and mom. What was the step-mom's name?"

"Maggie."

"Mom, this is her…." she said very slowly. That didn't register for a couple seconds. I had only taken pictures of our family that day at the graveyard. I was confused. Maybe she had been buried with Henry's family for some reason. Trying to control myself and not take her discovery away from her, I said, "Come sit by me and let's see what you have there." She got up and ran around the table with the black and white pages we had printed of the pictures. She plopped down beside me and pointed to the one of Maggie Dukes. "See!!" she exclaimed. I could see that her 10-year-old little self was about to explode. Maggie was not buried with Henry's family as I had thought was possible… She was buried with her parents for sure. I knew exactly who I was looking at…

"They were related." I exhaled, but how closely I wondered.

"Who is?" Felecia wanted to know.

"The dad and the step-mom," I said. "But I don't know how close."

"They were related to each other? Eeeewwww!" She was making a disgusted face. She made me laugh, which I had to stifle because we were still in the library.

"Be still now, you'll get us thrown out," I was smiling at her. She giggled. "Well, come on, let's figure out how they are related… It's killing me!" She was all smiles.

It only took a few minutes to figure it out. I got out the immediate family chart I had done some time back on Maggie's dad. His name was William Jackson Dukes. Maggie's dad and my great granddad were brothers. Henry and Maggie were first cousins. They were 82 and 80 when they were killed and had only been married a few years, so they were not going to have any children together, but, still, first cousins? That was just too close, I shivered.

"You ok?" Felecia asked. "Did you figure it out?" She was waiting patiently. *Almost.*

"No, you did!" I told her. "You figured it all out. I am pretty sure that this is what caused him to kill them." I slowly began to explain how they were related. Using her and her cousins as examples.

"Gross, I would never marry Evan. That's just weird!" she exclaimed.

"I know and I think that is what pushed him over the edge. I bet he was so ashamed. And the paper never said any-thing about them being related, so the cops would not have put that together either." I contacted my long-lost cousin at the Greenville Annex the next day and told her of our discovery. "You are kidding!" She gasped on the phone. "I never made the connection."

"I can't imagine anyone would. You would not think to see

if two married persons were related to one another in today's time." I explained. "I would not have either if Felecia had not noticed the death dates on the gravestone." She was very excited to have this news and promised she would contact the local paper to see if they would be interested in doing an interview for a public interest story to set the record straight. I gave her my thanks and we ended the call.

"I can't imagine what other skeletons I might find in our tree after a discovery like this one. Right off the bat, too." I told Felecia. Little did we know what we would unearth in just a matter of days...

Chapter 4

We had gotten several generations back on my mom's family and still had a little less than a year before her birthday. So, we had decided to take it out as far as we could go. "We may not get any further at all," I had said to Felecia, "but it would be silly not to try with this much time left to use." She agreed. We had finished with her schooling for the day and decided to sit in the living room floor and spread out all of our information and make a list of the things we would look for next. "We never did find Grandma's birth record," I said. "We should give that our full attention. Your Mamaw said that Grandma had been told her entire life that she was a twin, but, that her twin had died."

"Oh, that's sad." Felecia pouted.

"Yes, but they didn't have the doctor's knowledge and medicine like we do today." I explained.

"But still… and how did she not know for sure? That seems weird!" She was curious.

"Remember her mom died when she was really little and her oldest sister is the one that had tried to give her as much information as possible, but she was only 7 when Grandma was born and then their mom died five years later, and her dad would never talk about any of that stuff. Grandma said he was never the same after she died. Guess it was true love." "So anyway, her information was limited."

"Well, we have tried looking for it at the library, what can we do different to try to find it now?" she asked.

"Let's try the little old lady at the library, she is sure to know some tricks we have never heard of. I will call our new cousin at the Annex, she may know something about it. I never thought to ask her before." So, I grabbed the phone and dug through my purse to find the number and called the Annex. As luck was with me, she was working. I explained what I was needing, and she couldn't help. My grandmother wasn't in her direct family line, so she had never looked into her before. She wished me well and I hung up.

"No luck?" Felecia asked me.

"Nope, and it's almost five, too late to go to town now. We have to help Mamaw clean her house all day tomorrow… it's gonna have to wait until Friday."

"That stinks!" she exasperated!

"But!" I said, "this will be the perfect opportunity for you to distract her so that I can sneak out some of the pictures of her brothers and sisters!" She was smiling now. Good, I thought.

We woke up early the next morning and did a little school and then started getting ready to go to Mom's. "Don't forget your spelling words, your math workbook and the map of Africa. We will do that during lunch."

"How am I supposed to distract her?" She was obviously thrilled with the idea of being in on the scheme.

"Well, let's see, lunch would probably be best. We will all be sitting down, so I will say that I have to go to the bathroom, and I will really sneak into her library and get the pictures out of the photo album. *Yes, my mom has a library in her house. We LOVE books!* Just keep her focused on you, maybe you can ask her to drill you on your spelling words?"

"Hmmm, that doesn't sound like much fun…"

"Remember your being sneaky for me, that will make it fun."

"Ok." She said begrudgingly.

We grabbed our stuff and headed out the door. My parent's farm was only about 4 miles up the road from our house, so it was a short trip. We got out of the car and Mom was at the door calling to Felecia.

"How's Mamaw's girl this morning?" *Felecia and my mom were two peas in a pod. I am more like my dad and his side of the family. Mom and Felecia both love to read, and I mean LOVE. They just sit together for hours on end and just read. They are so cute together.*

"Hey, Mom!" said the chopped liver.

"Hello, how are you?" she asked me.

"Good, we got up a little early and did some schoolwork. But we will need to finish during lunch, should only take about an hour."

"Are you learning anything, Felecia?" Here we go...

"Mom, please don't worry, she is doing really well!" I was trying to use an even tone.

"Well, what do you think would happen if every child was home schooled?"

"Probably and lot more learning and a lot less sex on the school bus!" I chirped.

"Tonya, I never in all my days!!"

"It's ok, Mamaw. We are doing sex-ed this year. I know all about it!"

"JESUS, MARY & JOSEPH!" She wailed, covering her face with her hands. Felecia had always had the uncanny ability to make every conversation with my mother more interesting.

"Are we cleaning today or what? Let's get this party started!" I said smiling. She was glaring at me. *If looks could kill...*

"I will dust!" I exclaimed. I loathe dusting and Mom knew it, but I didn't want her to make me do it, so I may as well volunteer.

"I will run the sweeper!" Felecia burst out. Mom was just standing there dumb founded as we headed to the linen closet to get our tools.

A few hours later all three of us were ready for some lunch. Mom was making sandwiches and had made potato salad the day before.

"Mamaw, do you have some chips?" Felecia was making a face.

"Yes, Fle, Mamaw knows you don't like potato salad."

"Are the kids coming in from college for Thanksgiving?"

My step-niece and nephew go to school out of town and can't always make it in for the holidays. My stepsiblings are great people and we enjoy getting together. Felecia and my niece were born 4 days apart and my nephew was born exactly a year later. So, we always did all the birthdays together at my mom and stepdad's.

"No, your sister is going to have Thanksgiving with Michael in Bowling Green and Alex is staying in Chicago." She was putting mayo on our bologna and cheese. "Are you bringing the meatballs and green bean casserole?" She was walking toward the table now.

"Sure, whatever you need me to do." Which is why we were there today. She always does 'Fall cleaning' before the holidays. Ceiling fans, base boards, cabinets and windows, the whole shootin' match. *Ugh...*

"Just your usuals will be fine."

"Do you want me to make mac and cheese since Deb will be in Bowling Green?"

"Hmmm, I hadn't thought of that. Yea, that would be good."

"Felecia, if you are done, you need to get on your spelling words. I need to go to the bathroom." That was her que. I was walking out of the kitchen when I heard Felecia ask Mom to help her with her words. I walked straight into the library, didn't want to waste time. I found the photo album I knew had her old photos in it and started peeling them out slowly. My plan was to get them scanned and copies made and put them in a kind of scrapbook. Sort of 'This is your life' in book form. I found all the ones I needed and carefully put them in my back pocket. I would try to get them in my purse later. I peeked out into the hall and ran over to the bathroom. I went in, flushed the toilet and came back out. As I was coming down the hall, I heard Felecia spelling. Before I attempted to sit back down, I asked, "Are we ready to get back at it?"

"Yep, don't want to tarry too long." Mom said. I told Felecia to finish her studies and let me know when she was done. She nodded, then as soon as Mom started walking away, she gave me a questioning look and a thumbs up. I smiled and gave her a thumbs up. She was all grins the rest of the afternoon. We both knew that tomorrow we were going to the library and hopefully would be uncovering some lost information.

Chapter 5

'Woohoo, it's Friday' I thought as soon as my feet hit the floor. I made breakfast and got the hubby off to work, and Felecia and I went to the home school room in our jammies. "Let's get school behind us before we go to town today because neither of us will want to mess with it at the library. We will be too distracted!" She was nodding vigorously. English first, then history (our favorite), then math, and finally writing. *She had cursive mastered, but because of her dyslexia, she struggled with print. Weird right? And she was left handed just like my dad. The struggle was real...*

11:32 and we were walking into the library. Everybody knew us by now. Not by name but that we were regulars to the reference room downstairs. Just like 'Cheers', it is very comforting to go where everyone knows you. On the way down in the elevator I realized that I should have called to see who was working downstairs today. But too late for that. We walked in and saw most of the same faces as usual. There was my little old lady friend! She jumped up and hugged us both, "I was hoping I would see you today! You two always brighten my mood." *I could just eat her up she was so sweet.*

"What are you looking for today?"

"You probably don't remember, but we have never found my grandmother's birth record. And my mom says that Grandma was supposedly a twin and it didn't make it. We have searched through the Kentucky birth records every way but sideways but found nothing. Any ideas?"

"You're still on the Dukes', right?"

"Yep, but she was born a Browning."

"Oh, that's right! Takes a minute to get this old brain workin'." She winked at Felecia. "You haven't looked at the micro fiche?"

Apparently not because I had no clue what she was talking about. "No, what is that?" She was leading us to the other side of the room.

"This," she had her hands on a machine, "is the projector. And this little box holds all the records of births from 1911 to 1955."

"That little box has all that?" I was confused. The box was about seven inches tall and eight wide and maybe 5 deep. She opened it and pulled out a file. The words were so tiny I could not read it. I was squinting. She said,

"That's why you need the projector." She slid the file in, pointing out that it went in upside down and backwards, and turned on the switch. I could hear the host of heaven singing… It was amazing. Felecia and I were standing there with our mouths hanging open. She was giggling at us.

"Sorry," I said.

"Everybody does that the first time."

"Really?" I didn't feel quite so silly now.

"So, I just grabbed this one to show you how it works. The files in the back of the box are by the mother's name and the files in the front are by the individual's name. They are indexed in alphabetical order and numbered. I know you will want to find it yourself so if you need me, just come get me." I was so excited I thought I might burst. I grabbed a chair so Felecia could sit beside me and started looking through the files. Bourne, Bradford, Bretley… Browning! I put the file in the projector and the image came up. It was showing the D Brownings. Trying to drive this machine that had its contents upside down and backwards was not easy. In fact, it was difficult. Finally, I found the Gs and with a little more adjusting I had it. There she was!!!! But her birthday was wrong. I started talking to myself…

"Mother's name is on the far right." "Martha St…., that's not right her last name is spelled wrong!" "That's why we couldn't find her!"

"Shhh, Mom." Felecia said quietly. I hadn't realized I had

gotten loud.

"Sorry…" I was so excited. "Ok, I guess we will write down this information and then look in the mother's files and see if we can find a child with the same birth date as Grandma's. Can you write this down as I read it off?" She was all too eager to help. I recited the date, county, certificate number, volume number, and the way my great-grandmother's name was spelled. She got it all down. And then I went to the mother's names and looked for Stipworth instead of Skipworth.

"Found it!" I was stumbling with my hands I was trying to move so fast. Again, trying to move this dang thing the opposite direction my brain thinks it needs to go. "This is like trying to cut your own hair using the mirror!!" *Remain calm,* I was telling myself. "Here she is… there's Grandma and, (I was holding my breath) a baby boy with a death date the same as Grandma's birth date." My heart broke a little…

"Mom?"

"It's ok sweetie, I really didn't expect to find anything, so I am a little surprised that's all. His name was Garlen… Gracie & Garlen, that has a nice ring to it don't you think?" I was wishing that my Grandma was still with us. She was alive but senile dementia had taken her from us several years ago and she was in a local nursing home. *I would love to sit down and tell her about having a brother, but she would not even know who I was.*

"Let's go ask what we do now."

Chapter 6

I was beside myself wanting to know all the details. Why was her birthday wrong? She led us to a tall cabinet,

"All of the birth certificates are on film in this cabinet. The fiche is just the index to find out where and when. First look for the volume year and pull that roll out, you already know how to load it, and the certificates are in order. Did you find her?"

"Yes! It looks like she did have a twin brother. But her birthday is wrong."

"That happened more than not, all those years ago. They didn't have papers and things like we do now. It was just another day."

"Wow, that just seems odd to me."

"Yep, it does to most folks. Let me know if you need anything else." She walked away. I turned to look at Felecia.

"Ok, so what is the volume year?" "1912", she said. I found the roll I needed and loaded it into the viewer.

"And the certificate number?"

"25641!" I needed to scroll to about halfway through the roll. I was holding the button to fast forward and let up,

"25598, I guessed pretty close." I said smiling at her. "Grab that other chair so you can study it with me." I pressed the slow forward button for a few short bursts and let go, I was 3 off. I grabbed the roll and turned it by hand. "That's it!" I breathed out slowly. I think I was afraid I would wake up from a fantastic dream. Her name was at the very top. "Hmmm, it doesn't have her middle name." I looked down, "but there are her parent's names, so this is definitely her."

"Her middle name was Deweese, right?" I nodded in agreement. "It's right there." Felecia was pointing to the bottom of the certificate.

"Dr. C. W. Deweese." I was shaking my head. Then I started to giggle!

"What's funny?" she was looking at me like I had lost it.

"She hated that name, with a passion. And it wasn't even her real name. Her sister must have just knew she had heard it and figured it was just part of her name. This is cracking me up!" "And that is why her birthday is wrong, Ermon *(my great aunt)* just didn't remember it right. We have celebrated her birthday on Dec 7th my entire life and she was born in October. Let's see what else she got wrong." A little further down, it said, 'One of twins, born alive'. Wow… I bet that was heartbreaking to lose a baby you had carried the entire pregnancy. But back then she probably didn't even know she was carrying twins until the delivery. Garlen's certificate number was the one after hers, so I grabbed the roll and turned it. He didn't have a middle name either. 'Stillborn, one of twins born dead', there was more… 'both babies born before my arrival, mid wife stated deceased male child born first then contractions returned, and live female birth followed,' I know my mouth had to have been hanging wide open. It was like that phrase I had always heard, 'It was like a train wreck, but I couldn't look away.' I now understood that feeling. I was so sad for my great-grandmother but excited all at the same me. There was a print button right in my face, so I pushed it. Out came a perfect black and white copy. Then I backed up to Grandma's certificate and hit print again. My mom was not even going to believe this, I was having a hard time and I was looking at the evidence.

I had a missed call and a voice mail on my cell phone. I flipped it open, and the missed call was from the Annex in Greenville.

"Hmmm, that's weird. She has never called me before, must be important. You ready for a break? We can run upstairs and get some sunshine and I will listen to the message." We told our friend we would return in about 15 minutes and she asked if I could watch the room for her when I came back.

"We are short staffed today and I just need a short break. About 20 minutes, ok?"

"Sure, not a problem at all."

It was warm for early November and the sun felt wonderful on my face. Now, let's hear this message, I thought. "Hey, girl! It's your cuz at the annex. I have found something really interesting. Give me a call when you get a sec." Well, I was thinking, this is fixin' to get crazy. Because I had something interesting to tell her too. I looked over at Felecia, she was nose deep in a copy of 'The Boxcar Children', and I knew she wouldn't mind us being out here a few more minutes.

"Hey, it's Tonya. I listened to your voice mail. What's up?"

"I was doing research on our family and discovered that three sets of your 3x great grandparent were double first cousins! How cool is that?" She was obviously very excited and proud of her find, but I didn't really understand what she had said.

"Okay, you are going to have to either slow it down or dumb it down, because you lost me at 'double'. That is not a term I have heard before."

Okay, imagine a tree bracket and you are looking at the great-grandparent part… where there are four sets of couples…"

"Okay." I said.

"Now, two of the husbands and one of the wives were all siblings and the reverse for the spouses."

"So? Those 3 sets of people all came from 2 sets of people? And then their kids married each other?"

"Yep." She confirmed.

"Gross!" I was disgusted.

"Well now you have to remember that back in that time period, people didn't move around. They settled where they were and if all their relatives stayed around the same town also, eventually you began to run out of people you weren't related to… I mean the young men didn't hitch up the horse and buggy on Saturday night and drag Main Street looking for a date!

They met at church functions and town fairs and such."

"That is hilarious! And you're right, I never thought of it that way. But now I am seeing Amish looking guys in horse drawn buggies trying to pick up chicks in my head." I was laughing out loud.

"So, you got it straight then?" She wanted to verify before letting me go.

"Yes, but I have found something interesting, too. You got a couple more minutes?"

"Sure!"

"So, you know I couldn't find my grandmother's birth record or if she had been a twin or not..." I gave her the full story. She was interested but not as excited as me because my grandmother was not part or her direct line, but she was very glad for me to finally be able to close the door on that chapter. We parted with me saying, "I'll try to see you soon", and I hung up.

"You ready to get back inside, Sweetie? We have to watch the room, you know."

Chapter 7

We made our way back downstairs and relieved our friend for her break. There were only regulars in there at the time, so it wasn't necessary for me to do anything.

"Let's sit down and go over this new information. K?"

"I was reading and didn't even pay attention to what you were talking about," Felecia stated.

"Well, it is pretty confusing, so I was planning on putting it on a separate chart. It is too far out on our tree to fit on our current chart. Will you get us a new chart from the shelf, please?" She was back in a flash.

"Okay, so Elizabeth Ann Zeplhia Wells and John Perry Wells were brother and sister. And she said that they married siblings."

"Their own siblings?!" Felecia choked out.

"No, the people they married were siblings to each other." I started shuffling my papers around looking for what I needed. "Here we go, let's just write it out. So, Elizabeth married Starling Dukes and John married Mariah Dukes. But Starling and Mariah were not siblings... hmmmm." I was searching through my papers again and found our cousin's tree chart. "Here we go. John's first wife was Starling's sister. She died very young, and he re-married our ancestor, Mariah, second. So, in her direct line, they were double first cousins. But Starling and Mariah's fathers were brothers, so they were first cousins all ready." My head was starting to spin. This was a bit too confusing... and Felecia's face was all screwed up trying to follow me. I was writing it out to make it easier for us both.

"And, Starling and Elizabeth had William, and John and Mariah had Mary Frances and William and Mary married each other and they were second and third cousins!" I knew my mom was not going to like this part of her tree. But, hey, it's the past and we can't change it. So, it is what it is...

I found it all fascinating. I can only imagine what it would have been like to have lived back then. *I do, try to imagine what it was like for my ancestors.* They did not have it easy for certain. They struggled and worked hard for every little bit they had. I owe my entire existence to them. Murders, mistakes and mayhem... they were my blood, and I was proud to be one of them! I realized then, that I had started this for my mom, and I would give it to her for her birthday, as I had planned. But this was about me too now, and I would have to do my dad's side of the family for myself and Felecia. She deserved to know where we came from. Beans, taters and all. We had a lot of information that was for sure. When we left the library, we headed to the craft store. We needed a book and paper to start our project.

"How about I pick the book and you pick the paper?"

"Deal!" She exclaimed. It was raining and dreary outside.

"How about we get this stuff and go home and put her book together? As much as we can anyway, before I start dinner." She nodded agreeably. We pulled into the parking lot. And I grabbed the umbrella from the back seat. I got out and went around and got her. We huddled under the umbrella to try and stay dry. We got inside and shook like old dogs.

"It was so pretty earlier, I didn't know it was supposed to rain."

"Me either, but we will have fun when we get home!".

"Yep, so let's get what we need and head home. It will probably get cool soon, with this front coming in."

"What color book are you going to pick?" She was curious.

"Well, I'm thinking dark blue or grey. Nothing flashy. She will more than likely put it in the library.

"We got to the isle with the books, and I saw one that I liked with gold on the front, and it looked like leather." *I couldn't afford real leather.*

"Do you think it needs something on the front? I do, but I don't know what."

"I have no clue, Mom, you will have to do that by yourself. Where is the paper? I want to pick out something old timey looking. Is that okay?"

"I think that would be perfect. Should be right around the corner here." She spotted what she wanted immediately. Ivory with tiny, little, blue flowers and dark green leaves.

"How about this?!"

"Oh, I love it and so will Mamaw. I want to find some letters for the front, and we will brainstorm on the way home."

'Gold would be nice. That would match the front."

"That is a perfect idea. You are so Smart!"

We set straight to our task when we got home. Cutting and cropping pictures, deciding what should go where. What order? Garlen's birth/death certificate, I wanted on a page by itself. And the pictures I had found in the Dukes file at the Annex and the family book at our library. We were having a great time, stuff was scattered all over the living room floor.

"This is a ton of stuff, Mom. Her book is going to be awesome!"

"Yep, her family has left quite a legacy for us to find. THAT'S IT! A LEGACY... That's what is going on the front of the book!"

Chapter 8

A single tear spilled over her lower lid and rolled down her cheek and across the back of her hand. She cleared her throat and wiped the evidence of the tear away.

"Honey?" my stepdad was looking at her.

"It's my family, all of them, together, with their birthdays and my mom and dad… I don't know what to say." *(I had used a generic program on my ancient desktop to put all her pictures together to make it look like her, her 8 siblings and her mom and dad were all in one photo.)* She was looking at me now.

"Felecia and I have answered a lot of your family mysteries, Mom. I hope you like it." She couldn't speak, she was just looking at me. I reached out and patted her hand. "Felecia, do you want to show her Grandma's birth record?" She automatically turned the page. "See Mamaw, she was a twin!" Felecia was pointing at the record, and then she pointed to Garlen's.

"He died Mamaw… isn't it sad?" Mom's mouth was hanging open. She grabbed my hand and squeezed it hard.

"Oh, I wish we could tell her. She would have loved to have known what really happened."

"I know," I said, "I know."

We spent the next two hours going over all the details. Everything Felecia and I had found. The friends we made at the library and the new cousin at the Annex in Greenville. She was in awe, and she should be. I mean we had a couple years-worth of information to give her.

'I can't believe we celebrated her birthday wrong all those years!' and 'She would have been thrilled to know Deweese was not her middle name' and 'Mamaw, you had a relative named Joseph Caesar Sampson Columbus Dukes, and he named his son Fred and Mom thinks that is hilarious' me and mom laughed until we cried over that one and, Mom says we are so inbred we should have a third eye' That one she didn't think was quite as funny, but she laughed at Felecia none the less. The best part, *my favorite part,* was being able to use the library computer to build our tree on a famous genealogy site and finding other people who were very distant relatives that had uploaded pictures of my great grandparents and further back. Pictures that no one in my family had ever seen before. And a picture of my mom's dad's mother. She had died when my papaw was a baby. When mom got to her picture, she was thrilled.

"I guess you're sure it's her? I mean I don't want to doubt you, it's just I have wanted to know what she looked like my entire life. Dad didn't even remember what she looked like. He was so little when she died. And how did you get this picture of mom's mom? I knew her, but I have never seen this picture before."

"I called Aunt Bliflis *(my childhood version of Elizabeth)* to ask about anything interesting about your family and we chatted a bit and then she called me about three weeks later and said she needed my address. She said Randy *(my cousin)* had been in a lady's house doing some repair work on her floors because she had got a leak and it did some damage. He noticed an old picture and just commented about it. She said that it was her grandfather Ira Skipworth. Well, of course, he said his grandmother was Martha Skipworth and wondered if they were related. She just smiled at him as she was taking the picture out of the frame to show him that Martha was with him in the picture, she just had her covered up. They were brother and sister! So, they jumped in his truck and ran to town to get copies made. Aunt Bliflis mailed me a copy." Mom was just shaking her head. "That is amazing. I can't imagine the luck." She was just staring at the picture. I knew where my mom's beauty came from. Martha was stunning. Then my mom did the unthinkable…

"Did I ever tell you the story of how my mom and dad got

married?" You could have knocked me over with a feather.

"No!." So she began,

"Well, mom said that her mom and dad had thought she was too young to court much less get married, so she was told they would have to wait. I had no idea that she was only fourteen until today, she never told me. But they would leave love notes for each other in a hole in a tree in a field. And one day she opened her note from him and it said, 'Let's run away and get married' and that he would be back to the tree at a certain time with their friends for witnesses. 'If you really love me, you will be here', she showed up and they eloped to Rockport, IN, I know now. It is so fun knowing the facts behind the story. I never knew their age or where they got married. Much less that they had lied to do it." She was laughing.

"Well," I started, "I couldn't help but notice it was a little over two years before they had their first child. I wonder if he abstained..." I leveled my gaze at her and cleared my throat, "because maybe she was too immature just yet?" Mom was smiling a tme, she caught that I was being discreet in front of Felecia. "I'm sure you remember the story of my dad saying she played with dolls when they first got married," I was nodding my head, "You may be completely accurate about that." I shrugged my shoulders, one of those things we would never know for sure.

"There is an interesting story about Martha and Finis too." This was fantastic, Mom was actually sharing her stories with me. We had never done this before. I was thrilled.

"Oh yes, tell me!"

"Well, my mom had said that her mother's family was very well off. Extremely rich. And that if she persisted in wanting to marry a lowly farmer she would be disowned and written out of the will and be penniless. And we have been poor ever since!" She was laughing really hard. I was in shock again, she actually just said she had been poor. We for sure had never talked about that before. This was one of the best days of my life.

We talked a bit longer, then my stepdad said,

"Are ya'll gonna jaw jack all day or are we gonna eat? I'm starving!" We all started laughing because we were all starving and just failed to realize it. I helped Mom get the food together and Felecia set the table. We had roast beef and swiss on the 'good bread', her homemade potato salad and Felecia had chips. *She still doesn't like potato salad! LOL*

Chapter 9

We chatted light heartedly throughout lunch and then cleared the table.

"Did I ever tell you about Roger *(my mom's youngest brother, she practically raised him. They have a very special bond)* writing your dad a note?" I shook my head no.

"I was in the bathroom taking a shower, and he would come over every so often to stay the night after I married your dad. He missed me so much. So, your dad had to use the bathroom and he came in the bathroom while I was in the shower and Roger slid a note under the door to him. It said, 'You shouldn't be in the bathroom when my sister is in there too'! Is that not the funniest thing ever?" She was wiping tears away she was laughing so hard. We were all laughing hysterically, really, my uncle was so funny. I could just see him doing something like that.

I didn't want to leave, but I had to get home and get dinner in the oven. "Well Mom, I guess we better be getting home."

"Oh, Mom, do we have to go?"

"Do you want to stay the night with Mamaw? I can take you to church with me or drop you off at home before church, whichever you want, Tonya."

"Oh Mom! Can I please?! Please, please!"

"Ok. But she needs to come home before church. She needs to be in our children's church because they are getting ready for their play."

"I almost forgot!" Felecia said.

"That's not a problem." Mom said.

"Ok then, I will see you in the morning, sweetie." Hugs, kisses and goodbyes.

Less than 5 minutes later, I was home, all by myself! I grabbed the phone and called my dad. My stepmom answered.

"Hi Honey, what are you doing?"

"I have decided to do Daddy's family tree and I have a ton of questions."

"Well, he is out in the Florida room, hang on just a second."

"Hi Sug. Wha'cha doin'?"

"Hi Daddy! I'm needing some information about your family. I want to do your tree. Can I bend your ear a bit?"

"Sure, ask away!"

I started with my great-grandparent's info. I knew nothing about them. Names, birthdays, locations and his siblings that had passed away when they were young.

"I can't remember if it was Dad's mom or Mom's mom, but she was a Cherokee princess." Hahaha, not likely I thought. *I have never seen an Indian with an afro, but no need to go there right now.* My dad was 1 of 16 kids… what were they thinking. I can't imagine. But they kept having kids to work the farm. And with my mom being 1 of 9, I had so many cousins I didn't know half of them. Family reunions were crazy! "Your Grandpa Joe was in the Navy."

"No way! I didn't know that."

"I would love for you to find out about that, he never talked about it. I don't know how long he was in, or if he even fought. Can you look into that?"

"Sure, Daddy. I don't know how to start but I will find out. Anything else?"

"You should call Barbara and Margaret. They have way more info than I do. And one of them has a picture of Daddy in his Navy uniform. I'm sure you could get a copy."

"Are you serious? I have never even seen a picture of Papaw when he was young, much less in uniform! I have Aunt Margaret's number, but I don't think I have Aunt Barbara's. Can you give it to me?"

"Yep, I have it right here. You ready?"

"Yep!" After I had the number, I told him I would probably call him a hundred more times in the next few months. He thought that was fantastic.

"Tell Jax I love her and Amy, and I love you too, Daddy!"

"Love you too, Sug."

While I was on the phone with him, I thought that I should call the Annex and see what they have on Daddy's side of the family.

"Hey, cuz! How are things at the Annex today?" I chirped to my new cousin.

"Slow for a Friday, but the weather forecast called for rain here today, so the older ladies probably made plans to stay home. What do you have going on today, Tonya?" She asked.

"I have decided to do my dad's family tree and was wondering if you had a file on them before I make the trip down?"

"What was your grandfather's name again, I know you told me before, but I have forgotten?"

"Joe Edison Avery."

"Oh, that's right and yes we have a file. I wanted to tell you before, but I know me and if you are like me, you would have wanted to look at it right away and would have gotten yourself all confused!"

"You are right about that! Is there very much in there?'

"Quite a bunch, actually. When will you be coming? I would like to be here so I can see you?" "Well, what is your schedule next week?"

"I will be here every day but Thursday. I have an appoint ment."

"Let's say Tuesday then. Sound good? It will be after lunch so we can get school done for the day."

"Great! I can't wait to see you. I want to hear about your mom's tree and what she thought, but I have a customer needing me. So, I will see you Tuesday!"

"Fab, see you then!" I was ten kinds of excited! I just couldn't wait to see that file.... Better call Aunt Margaret now, I was thinking to myself, I will have to start dinner soon.

Chapter 10

"Hi! Uncle Darrel? Is Aunt Margaret home? It's Tonya!"

"Sure! Hang on a sec while I get the phone to her... how have you been? Heard from your dad lately?"

"Yep, I just talked to him a little bit ago. He's mean as ever!" Uncle Darrel was laughing at me.... *One of those deep down in your gut kinda laughs. He was such a sweet man; I thought the world of him.*

"Here she is Tonya!" I heard her say, 'Tonya?' in the background, and then...

"Well, I'll be!! I haven't heard from you in a coon's age! How you doin' honey? Have you talked to your daddy lately? He doin' ok?" *My dad was a very bad diabetic and he was notorious for not taking care of himself. He worried his sisters to death.*

"He is good! I just talked to him about an hour ago. I had lost your number and called him to get it. He said when I called you to tell you that he loves you all and they are gonna be home in August and will make a trip to visit."

"Well, you make sure you come with him and bring that baby girl so I can spoil her! I just love to play with her hair, ya know."

"Hahahah, I know you do... and we will. I promise. I have started a project and I need your help, if you have the time to chat?"

"Well sure, honey. Wha'cha into?"

"I am going to do your family tree. I have just finished my mom's and now I want to do Daddy's. I need to pick your brain." So, I started with the usual stuff, had my tree out in front of me and started filling in the blanks as she feed me the information. Just like my mom, she didn't know very far back. But anything was better than nothing, Guess back in the day, people didn't talk a lot about this stuff.

"Great! All of that is going to be a big help. Now.... do you know any interesting stuff about us or funny stories or anything else I might like to know?"

"Well, you know Momma carried a 2-shot Derringer in her apron pocket. I remember you bein' at her house once when she shot it over Lloyd and Charlie's heads because they were fighting in the front yard!" Um, yes, I will never forget that. "And then there was that one time that they hitched a ride into town and stole a VW Bug and they took a chain saw to it because they wanted it convertible." I remembered that story too. "It's a wonder they didn't put Momma and Daddy in an early grave with the stunts they pulled."

"Did you know the first five cars daddy gave me were stolen?" I couldn't help but giggle as I told her...

"That don't surprise me at all! Glad you never got caught, I would have had to beat his behind! Oh! I have a picture of Daddy in his Navy uniform! And when we were little, this nice older couple lived across the road from us, and she lined us all up and took our picture one time. I never got a copy of it, but her kin still live around here. That would be a great find, your dad was about three or four and if I remember right, we looked like rag-a-muffins. Clothes all torn and faded... Lord help us... we were so poor." I had tears pricking my eyes, the thought of my daddy at three was enough but to think of him in tattered clothes was almost more than I could bear. I faked a sneeze so I could clear my throat.

"Daddy told me about Papaw being in the Navy and yes I would love to get a copy of that picture!"

I was pretty sure a month had gone by waiting for Tuesday to hurry up and get here. But finally, it had arrived. Felecia was spending the day with my mom, so I was off by myself. I had made a list of everything I wanted to try and find at the Annex, and plenty of change for copies. I had found a few things on the internet prior to today, so I had those with me for verification from my aunt. Oh, how I hoped I would be able to get a copy of that photo of my dad when he was little. It would be a prized possession.

My cousin had called me the night before to let me know they were anxiously awaiting my arrival and she had already taken several photos to get copies for me. She had the info on the family that may still have a copy of the picture of my dad. She said we could run over to their house after my visit with her mom. I could hardly control myself, I mean, what if they still had it? *Chances were slim, but hope is free!*

When I walked through the door of the Annex, my cousin was prepared to hug me tight. *These relationships I had developed were so dear to me now. I couldn't imagine my life without meeting them or the stories they had added to my life.*

"How are you?" She was beaming at me.

"I'm good, and you?"

"Same 'ole." She laughed. I got the file out for you this morning because I knew you would be coming in. I flipped through it, but nothing jumped out as overly exciting. But I don't imagine you need much more excitement, do ya?" We were both laughing now. "Go on over, (she was pointing to one of the tables) and I will check with you in a little bit."

"Super! Thanks." I sat down and opened the file. She was right, nothing extraordinary... until, my grandparent's marriage certificate. I had not found this yet. And it says my grandpa was divorced. No way... well that was something. I didn't know that. I will remember to ask about divorce records. A page was stapled to it. Two notes were copied on one sheet of paper with a message. 'Notes from parents for permission to be married, bound in the marriage book at the courthouse.' Oh, my goodness! I had to walk over to the courthouse right now!" I ran past the front desk, "Gotta run over to the courthouse, I'll be right back!" She didn't even have time to say bye and I was out the door. I was out of breath when I got to the top of the stairs. I better calm down, I'm not used to this kind of excitement, *I'm too chubby to get that worked up.*

I walked into the records room, "I'm wanting to look at

your marriage records please."

"Give me just a minute and I will walk you down." *Oh, good grief, lady! I am about to blow a gasket, I was thinking.*

"Ok. You ready?" *YYYEEESSSSSSS!!!!!!!!!!!!*

"Yes ma'am. Whenever you are." We were walking down a very narrow concrete staircase.

"Be careful. It can be a little tricky down these steps. The jail used to be down here years ago and now we use it for storage. Are you looking for something in particular?"

"Yes, my grandparent's marriage. I was told their parents hand wrote notes and, they are bound in the book with the certificate."

"Oh, my goodness, yes, we have several of that sort of thing in the older books. Well, I will find it for you. We try to maintain the integrity of the books, not that you would be destructive, we just have to be certain."

"Oh, that is not a problem. I understand completely." *I wanted to touch those notes so bad I could hardly control myself and if someone had torn them out or something, I would have just been devastated.*

"Let's see then. Look at you, you have the date and everything with you already." I had handed her the paper I had wrote it down on. "Okay, here is the index. And we are looking for book 12, which is right over here. Page 72.... Here we go! And there are your notes!"

"Can I touch them?"

"Oh honey, bless your heart, your tearin' up on me. Yes! You can touch them, but can you try not to get your tears all over everything?" I was not going to make any promises. I just couldn't believe it. The actual signatures of my great-grandparents. The notes looked like brown paper bag that had been torn. The notes were written in pencil. 'I give my permission for Joe Avery to wed Ms. Piper. Sam J. Avery' I ran my finger over his signature. "My daughter, Zella Mae can marry Joe E. Avery. Rosie Piper'. I was absolutely overjoyed.

"Would you like a copy?"

"Oh, yes, please. The copy I had seen was very faded. I want to share this with my family."

"Well, seein' as how this was such a special occasion for you. How 'bout I make you about 5 copies?"

"Oh, thank you so much. I will be glad to pay for all of them."

"No, this is free copy Tuesday. Didn't you know?" She winked at me.

Chapter 11

I went back over to the Annex, and finished looking at the Avery file. And like she had said there wasn't too much that stood out. I showed my cousin the copy of the notes and we added one to the file. This copy was a lot less faded. So, she threw the other one out. I told her I had to get if I was going to visit with my aunt, and I was off. I was just about to the house. I was thinking to myself… I don't have any close family, like siblings, I have a stepsister that I love dearly, but she lives in Florida with my dad and stepmom and I don't see her much. I need to make a genuine effort to see my relatives more. They will not be around forever, and family was beginning to mean more to me the deeper I dug into our heritage. My aunt was sitting outside on the porch waiting for me. She was grinning from ear to ear, she was truly happy to see me! What a great feeling… I couldn't even remember when I saw her last. I felt ashamed of myself… that's it! I will make time for my family from now on, and my next visit will be with Felecia! She was hobbling toward me as I was getting out of the car. All the women in my dad's family have leg problems, including me. She had snatched me up before I had shut the door behind me. She looked so much like Grandma, I teared up. She had been gone for a while now. I missed her so. She was a mess and a half, no doubt about that. My aunt had me by the face now, looking me over, still all smiles. "You look good!" She was beaming at me. By this time my cousin had realized I was there and was coming out the door.

"What up, Cuz!" *I have hundreds of cousins, but I had only spent a lot of time with just a few of them. And Tammy was one I was very close too*

"Gosh, it has been too long!" I said as I wrapped my arms around her. "I won't let it be so long again, I promise!"

"Good grief, you look like Mom!" She had taken a step back. "Don't you think she looks like pictures of you when you were younger?" She was asking her mom.

"I always thought she favored JoNell." Aunt Margaret was saying about her sister. I had never met her; she had died in a car wreck before I was born. We were walking into the house now.

"Grandma called me JoNell every time she saw me right before she died." They had both stopped and were just looking at me. My aunt was a little misty-eyed. Tammy recognized the need to change the subject and said,

"I can't wait to show you the pictures we have for you!" Me either, I was thinking! Tammy and I sat on the couch and Aunt Margaret sat in her special lift chair and I unrolled my tree. 2 feet by 3 feet, it consumed her coffee table and we dug in. *It is so funny, but you can ask someone, 'What do you know about your family?' and they always say not much. But when you get into it, they know a lot more then they realize.* So, my aunt was a wealth of knowledge, she had no idea how much she had retained of what my grandmother had told her over the years. I had to scoot down to the floor so I could write on my tree on the coffee table. She was handing me photos and saying this is so and so and this was your great such and such and on and on! I was on cloud nine!! "And this is mom's mom." She was saying. This woman was wearing a headdress! This is the source of my dad thinking his grandmother was an Indian.

"So, you think she was an Indian?" I was asking my aunt.

"Well, the proof is in the puddin'!" She was holding up the picture, with a very enthusiastic look on her face. I didn't want to burst her bubble, but unless my great-grandmother was also related to Minnie Pearl, I was pretty sure I could see a price tag hanging from the headdress in the bottom corner of the picture, which could have been taken at any carnival or traveling road show.

"Awesome!" was all I replied. *What I did find out about my great grandmother, later on, was astonishing.*

"Aunt Margaret. Do you know anything about Papaw being married before he married Jukey?"

"Yep. Supposedly his Daddy's best friend's daughter found herself in the family way, as they used to say. And the friend asked my grandad if he would have Daddy marry her and then divorce her, so as not to disgrace their family name. There have been rumors through the years that the boy was really his and they had really been in love, but I don't know that to be true or not."

"I was just curious because I found his marriage record to Jukey and it said he was divorced. Oh my goodness, I almost forgot I have a copy of something for you!" I gave her the copy of the notes and told her how I found them. She asked Tammy to take her to see it. She was ecstatic. I told her about the stairs and that she may need to go as soon as possible.

Chapter 12

Tammy asked me if I was ready to get this show on the road and I said, "Yes, I am! Let's roll out!" I was giggling at the excitement I felt! We weren't even out of the driveway yet, and all I could do was giggle. Tammy was driving,

"You excited or what?" She was laughing at me.

"I can't help it!" I blurted out. "This is a grand adventure for me, this whole thing has been really. All of the long-distance relatives and connections I have made. And now realizing how much I have missed my family. I won't go so long without seeing you guys again, that's for sure."

"Yep, it's crazy how busy we can all be and then you have to stop, take a breath, and slow down or the important things in life will pass you by." I was nodding in agreement. "Jukey always said life is what happens while you're while you're making plans!"

"Do you know these people? I mean, where we're going."

"Sure, I have seen them at church and around town." She was smiling. "They are a good bunch." *(You have to realize, that country people know others differently than we do. City folk have to KNOW someone before they say, 'I know them', country folk just have to basically know where they live. Because everyone talks to everyone about everyone else...)*

"They live up on the highway across the bridge from where Papaw Joe and Juckey used to live." Oh, I thought to myself, I knew exactly where that was. That meant we would be there in like two minutes.

"What's their name," I asked her, "I haven't even asked?"

"Duvall. But it's just the wife, her husband died about three years ago. It's a good thing all this came up now because she isn't going to be around much longer. She's real old." I suddenly realized we had turned the wrong direction.

"Are we going a different way?"

"I forgot to tell you, I'm sorry, Mom called her and told her we were coming by and asked if she needed anything. Mrs. Duvall asked if we could bring her a Milky Way. She told Mom that, 'She was havin' a hankerin' for some chocolate someth'n fierce'." Wow! Not only did I feel like I was being tortured, but my cousin had never even talked to this woman before, and we were making a trip to the store for her! My emotions were all over the place. *I was rapidly learning the kind of person I wanted to be...*

"Wait here and I will leave the car runnin' while I grab her candy bar. Want anything?"

"Diet anything would be good."

"Be right back!" I was so happy I could just cry! I loved my family! That may sound silly, but it was truly a revelation. I mean I knew I loved them because they were my family. But now I was realizing that there was depth to that love, something I could touch and see, because they have loved me this way all along and I never knew. She was back in the car. And we were on our way, once again. "I figured you would have exploded while I was gone, you looked so deflated when I said we had to run to the store." She was laughing at me again.

"I managed to control myself, thank you very much!" Now we were both laughing. We chatted light heartedly like it had only been a couple days since we had seen each other last and not years. So many years, I could not really remember the last time. And then we were pulling up in front of the Duvall house.

Chapter 13

The house looked abandoned, the yard was two feet tall, three in some places, all the paint was peeling off the siding, one of the windows was even broken with plastic over it. I must have looked shocked because Tammy was smiling at me.

"Mom said I wasn't allowed to be mad at her when I saw the house, dad came by here the other day and said he was comin' with the bush hog this weekend and some plexiglass to repair that window. She said Mrs. Duvall made a stink because he has his own family to take care of and he told her to hush 'cause she wasn't big enough to stop him. Mom said he is gonna look around and check it all out to see if there is anything else that needs fixin' before winter comes on." *Again, Wow!* She knocked on the door. I could hear movement and the house seemed to be moving as well. She flung open the door with such excitement that I nearly fell off the porch. No worries in falling though, before I knew it, she had snatched me up and was hugging me like she had known me forever. Then she turned me loose and had Tammy in a bear hug. I loved her already. Short and very round, just like Jukey, she waddled just like her too, but she had the blackest hair I had ever seen. She caught me staring,

"Somethin', ain't it? I have maybe 3 gray hairs and that's it. Ain't never dyed it and I reckon it'll still be black when the good Lord takes me to my husband. Not bad for 87, huh?" She had her hands on her round hips and was smiling from ear to ear.

"Well," I said, "I am only 35 and have been coloring my hair for years. Half my head is gray!" "Me too," Tammy said. We were all laughing. Tammy handed her the candy bar and she patted Tammy's cheek affectionately and just smiled. "Y'all sit and tell me what's on your mind." Tammy nudged me, "This is your adventure!"

"I was told by Aunt Margaret that you may have a photo that was taken by your mom about 1960's-ish (I was rocking my flat hand side to side to indicate my uncertainty) and I was hoping to get a copy of it to share with all of his siblings. She looked very confused. "Who's your momma, child?" She asked me.

"No, it was my dad. I'm Bill Avery's daughter."

"Little Billy?" Her mouth was hanging open. "Come here child and let me look at you!" I got up and walked over to her chair, she motioned for me to come down to her level, so I knelt on the floor in front of her. She leaned in real close and just studied me. "Well, you're not Lottie June's daughter, that's for sure. Who's your momma?"

"Carolyn Dukes. Who's Lottie?" I wanted to know. I had never heard that name before...

"Billy's first wife. Didn't you know your daddy had been married before?" She was wrong, had to be. I didn't want to be rude, but I didn't know what to say. I turned my head and Tammy was just looking at me and then started chewing on a fingernail. Well? My eyes were asking her.... Slowly she nodded her head in agreement. What? How could I not know this... I was floored!

"I'm sorry, child. I didn't mean to hurt your feelin's if I did."

"We had no idea that you didn't know...",Tammy managed to sqeake out.

"No, it isn't your fault at all. I would ask daddy myself if I could see him."

"Oh no, child. He's passed on then?"

"No ma'am. Last year he moved to Florida with my step-mom and stepsister. We are not real close. He left me and my mom a lot when I was growing up."

"Now I feel even worse, I'm so sorry."

"No, it's fine, really. I will ask my mom for sure when I get home." Now she was looking at Tammy.

"I will tell her the rest when we get back to Mom's." There's more? I was thinking… I need an aspirin, before we do all that... Then I thought again.

"No, I want to know now. Will you tell me now?" I was looking at Tammy.

Mrs. Duvall spoke up, "Oh I just feel awful! I didn't mean to cause a problem."

"No, Mrs. Duvall, it's not your fault. They should have told me. I am an adult, and they obviously had their reasons, but I need to know." I was smiling at her.

Tammy took a deep breath. "Well, he was married twice before your mom and you have two half brothers. One with each of his ex-wives."

"Brothers?!" I squeaked out loudly. "I have brothers?" Tammy was only four years older than me, but suddenly she had taken on a motherly tone.

"This is not the place to lose your mind, Tonya! The younger one is a decent guy, but the oldest, Darrell, is in and out of jail. He's a troublemaker."

"So, the older one is named after Daddy? He used to tell me, all the time, that he wished I had been a boy. And he had two, what was the problem there?" I was getting heated. I could feel the frustration welling up inside me. "That's jacked up, he deprived us all from a life with siblings..." I was shaking my head to myself, not able to understand.

"Well, actually, they were both named after him." Tammy said quietly.

"Ok?" It was more of a question than a statement. Mrs. Duvall was holding her breath, I was sure of it. *Please don't pass out now, I thought, I will never get the rest of this story if we have to call 911.*

"Until Scott changed his name, they were both named William Darrell Avery Jr." Tammy said, like she was afraid I might strike her. I was on my feet instantly.

"Are you kidding me!? Am I trapped in an "80's TV sitcom? 'Hi, this is my brother Darrell and my other brother Darrell'!"

I stammered mockingly. I was pacing the floor now, in a perfect stranger's house, fuming, no seething was closer to it. Mrs. Duvall leaned in and whispered to Tammy,

"What's a sitcom?" I burst out laughing hysterically... Sometimes in life you gotta laugh or you'll cry... So why not both? They were both laughing with me now. I was crying I was laughing so hard. We laughed until our sides were aching.

When we were able to compose ourselves again, I asked Mrs. Duvall if she thought she might still have that old photo. She was pretty sure she did. We searched for probably two hours before we found it. It was of daddy, Aunt Barbara and Aunt Ollie. Tammy's mom wasn't in the photo. *Funny how things get remembered wrong.* The sight of it made me cry. I don't think I was prepared for the poverty the picture showed. My heart was broken for him. I could not hold a grudge against him, when he was not here to defend himself. We helped Mrs. Duvall with a few things around the house, changing light bulbs, sweeping down cobwebs, and cleaning behind some heavy furniture. We left there feeling good, but I had a lot on my mind. It was close to ten years before I ever said anything about any of this to my mom. I think I felt I wasn't ready for it. The only reason I did then, was because I met Scott. But there will be more about him later...

Chapter 14

The last thirty minutes were a blur. I was driving home now, and I know I told my aunt goodbye, I just didn't remember. My head was spinning. Too much information, I couldn't process it all. Why had they never told me… I just didn't understand. I was hurt and angry at the same time. I'm going to keep this to myself, I was thinking. I wanted more details before I shared this with Felecia. I was going to pick her up from Mom before I went to get copies made of the picture of Daddy. She would be thrilled with all of the pictures Tammy had already made copies of and given to me. She would be my happy thought for today… I needed one.

She must have seen me pulling into the restaurant parking lot, because she came out to meet me.

"Are you hungry?" She asked. "Mamaw said we should have dinner here; they are not busy, and she can visit with us." I was hungry. I had so much on my mind that I had not realized that my stomach was growling.

"Sure, I won't have to cook!" It was going to be difficult to look at her and not be frustrated… but there had to be a reason, so I would have to grab my big girl panties and wait. She was sitting at the back table waiting for us to come in. My diet cola was already waiting for me in my usual spot. The waitress got our order and took it to the kitchen.

"Where's Fudd?" I asked her.

"He and Uncle Fuzz are bringing in the hay. So how was your visit? Did you learn anything interesting?" *OH, BOY, DID I!!* I was thinking…

"I got some really great pictures!" I was spreading them out on the table for them to see. Mom instantly zeroed in on the one of daddy when he was little.

"Wow!" She breathed out slowly. "I have never seen this picture before." I gave her a brief description of my visit at Mrs. Duval's house.

"He was so cute." Felecia was starring at the picture. "His outfit has hole in it, Mom."

"I know, honey, it was a long time ago. They were very poor."

"Well, he was one of sixteen kids!" Mom said. The sound of her voice brought back my frustration...

"Why would anyone have sixteen kids? Good grief!" Felecia was shaking her head.

"Your great Aunt Margaret said they kept having kids to help work the farm. My dad only went to school through the third grade and then he was made to stay home and help with the farming."

"Wow... that's crazy!" Felecia said.

"Well, it seems crazy to us, but that was a different time in the world. People did things a lot different than we do now. As a matter of fact, Felecia, he can't read or write. He is color blind and lefthanded, just like you. Which got him spanked in school a lot. But, when I graduated high school in 1986, he was making $22.00 an hour at the coal mine in Lynnville and that was excellent money for any man then. Much less a man with no education"

"So, how did this Mrs. Duvall come to have that picture of your dad?" Mom asked.

"She lived across the road from them when he was that little. Her mom is the one who took the picture. She still lives in the same house. She was quite a character. I want to visit her again soon. She was a wealth of knowledge."

"Hmmm, that little old house across the road from Joe and Jukey's place? I would have thought that had feel in a long time ago. Of course, I haven't been out there for years and years. And you and Tammy just went over?" *City folks!*

"Yes, we went and got her a candy bar and drove right over. And then we changed some light bulbs, moved furniture and swept down some cobwebs. Uncle Darrell is going over in a few days to mow and make some window repairs. Tammy had me in tears most of the entire time."

"The two of you always did get on well. So, Darrell knows this woman pretty well then?"

"No. Tammy said they had never really spoken to her before I asked about the picture. When she said that her husband had passed, they figured she needed some help getting the house ready for winter. Fle, we need to get going."

"Will she be coming over here after school tomorrow?"

"Nope. She has a diabetes appointment in Louisville to-morrow at 10am. So, she won't go to school at all tomorrow."

"Oh crud! I had forgotten about that." Felecia exasperated. "I was asking because I wanted her to stay the night tomorrow if you don't already have plans."

"No. I wanted us to go to the library after we get back to town, to do some more research. I can bring her by here around 5. That be ok?"

"Sure, that will be just fine!" Felecia was doing her happy dance, which always reminds me of Snoopy. We were both laughing at her now. I love you's and goodbyes…

Chapter 15

I had nearly forgotten that I wanted to get copies made of a few of the photos I had promised to return to Aunt Margaret. I told Felecia we were going to run out to the drug store to use the kiosk and then we were going home.

"Can I help!?" She asked eagerly.

"Sure. I always appreciate your help." She had a huge grin. And I wasn't kidding. She really was my helper... and my buddy, my partner in crime, my everything. Since my divorce, I had been having trouble getting myself together. I went through a wild tear for a short time, but now it was about us.

We walked into the store and I was rattling off more of my visit in Muhlenburg to her. The way Mrs. Duvall's house had looked. And how sweet she was, that she had known our family forever and the bear hugs. Felecia asked questions periodically and enjoyed helping me with the photocopies. We chatted the entire way home. When we got home, she put on her jj's, brushed her teeth, and I kissed her goodnight after prayers. I went to my room and got ready for bed, brushed my teeth, laid down and cried myself to sleep.

I felt so much better after a good night's sleep and the tears had erased a lot of tension. *Sometimes you need a good cry, you know?* It was about 7:00 am and we were headed to see the #1 pediatric endocrinologist in the state of KY. Daddy hadn't controlled his type 1 diabetes very well, he had been insulin dependent since he was 19. I had type 2, and just took a pill to control mine. Juvenile type 1 was something altogether alien to me. But he was fantastic and had made Felecia's type 1 diabetes not nearly as scary as it had been in the beginning. We had a routine with these visits. As soon as we were done with the doctor, we would drive about three blocks down the street and get some sliders and fries and then we would head home.

As soon as we got in the car, I told Felecia, "We need a list!" I am a list person. When going on a trip, I make a list of what lists I need before I start to pack. Today's list needed to be what all we needed to look for when we got to the library back home. She was getting a note pad and pen from the glove box.

"Ready!" she proclaimed. She loved writing my lists as I would dictate and ask her what else as we would brainstorm.

"Aunt Margaret said that Papaw Joe had been married before and wanted me to see what I could find out about who and when. She said he was very secretive about it. So that needs to go on the list. Daddy had two baby sisters that died when they were little. I want to find their birth and death records. Oh, and I want to check the newspaper database and see if there is anything about Jonell's wreck too."

"When was that?" She asked me.

"Hmmm, I am not sure. I wasn't born yet so before 1968. We will look for her death record also. Her last name was Hamby then because she was married. Oh yea, I forgot to tell you that my grandma had a nick name I had never heard either. Poke salad Annie. It was an Elvis song about a mean woman, and people used to call Jukey that when she was younger… I want to search for the words to that song and print them. I have never heard it."

"That's weird. I guess she really was mean." She was making a face. I was laughing at her.

"She may have been, but she was always good to me!" I patted her on the leg. We put a few other things on our list and chatted easily the rest of the trip. We got a double thumbs up from the doctor. She was doing excellent he said. We went and got our lunch and headed home.

We walked into the library and both of us inhaled deeply, we always do, instinctively. And then we always smile. We just love the library… Anyway. We walked into the reference department and I got an internet pass to access the library version of the genealogy site I use. We sat down and Felecia was trying to organize our list.

"I have a message!" I whispered. We were both big eyed, looking at the PC.

"I wanted to ask you about Joe Edison Avery. The 1920 census I found does not mention him under the Samuel Avery household despite the fact he was born in 1917. The 1930 census records him as being part of the Samuel Avery household right under Charles Avery. Was Joe Edison the youngest of the Avery siblings? Or a child of Charles? Thanks!"

"Get out of town! That is very cool." I had never even entertained the thought that someone might be researching the same family as me. "Well let's send her a message back." I told her about him living with his Aunt when he was young and her name. I explained my relation to him and ask if she was a relative or just doing research. I also told her how excited I was to get a message from someone as I was fairly new to the genealogy community. I absolutely could not wait to hear back from her.

Chapter 16

We set about checking things off our list. All the death records were easy and the birth records too. I could find nothing on Papaw Joe's first marriage. I mean nothing. I was beginning to wonder if it had been annulled. That would result in not being able to find anything. Like it never happened. But we were not Catholic, so that seemed doubtful. *Curious...*

There was nothing in the local newspaper from 1962 about Jonell's accident either.

"I guess that will be something to look for at the annex in Greenville. I know it will be there because it happened there."

"Well, we have done everything on the list, mom. What now?"

"We should try to dig a little deeper on Papaw Joe's side. My aunt knew nothing beyond his parents, Samuel Jackson Avery and Mary Jane Elizabeth Scifers. Or Sifers, Sciphers, Siphers, Cyphers or the other 5 ways we found it spelled. We need to find a way to narrow the search options. Let's ask and see if she has any ideas." We walked up to our little old lady friend. She had been swamped since we came in but was sitting back at the desk now.

"Well, hello! How are my two favorite girls today?" She is so cute I could just squeeze her!   "We are good! But I have a question."

"Shoot!"

"Is there any way to narrow a search if a surname is spelled twenty different ways? I am losing my mind with this one."

"That actually happens a lot. Especially with a name that is unusual. Most people didn't know how to read or write, and if they did, they were not great at it. You have seen the census records, half the time you can't read them. I guess I have never showed you the Soundex?"

"No, that's a new one."

"Well, it basically is for your problem. Census records were re-organized by the sound of the name…" She was shuffling through papers on her desk. "Here it is! This is the key for the Soundex, but the short of it is that they took out the consonants and sounded out the name using only the vowels sounds." We had been walking toward a cabinet. "Use the key to find out which roll of film to start with and go from there. You already know how to load the film but let me know if you need anything else."

"Well, isn't this nifty?" Felecia was obviously impressed.

"Who would have thought they would have a fix for this exact problem? Must have happened a lot or they would not have cared to fix it." She was watching me using the key.

"So… I is our first vowel sound and then E I guess for the ER sound." I was looking at the drawer labels and pulled out the one we needed. "Roll 1746, 1880. Here it is! Let's load it and see what we have." Felecia pulled up a chair so we could both sit in front of the projector.

"We don't know her dad's name, so I guess we are looking for her as a kid right?"

"Yep, and my goodness there are a ton of A's. But none of them have a Mary Jane Elizabeth for a child." We had been looking for quite some time when we both pointed to the screen.   "That has to be her, Mom!"

"Yes, it does. But they are all initials. Guess the census taker couldn't spell very well. Her dad is C. Scifers, mom is W. C., two stepsons, H. and J. T. Kesinger, and M. J. E. Scifers."

"It says she is seven and her mom has already lost a husband? Good grief, this stuff can be depressing." She was making a face.

"I'm sure life was extremely difficult back then. But now we know where to start. We will see if we can find a marriage record for her and her first husband. Do you remember where the books are for Grayson County?" She was nodding vigorously. "Go grab the marriage index that will have the 1850's and 1860's, and we'll see if we can find a Kesinger marrying a W. C. anybody shortly before the birth of the oldest son." When she returned with the book, I was adding C. Scifers and W. C. to our tree and she already had the book open looking. "Here he is! John Kesinger to Winifred C. Logsdon, Jan. 25, 1865. And it says that Harrison Logsdon was his surety. I wonder if that could be her dad?" She was very excited.

"Well, he is obviously her relative, so it is very possible. Great job, honey! So, I guess I am headed to the county seat of Grayson. But today was my last day off for a while so I will have to wait a bit to find the answers we need."

Chapter 17

About four months had passed since we had made our discovery about Winifred Logsdon. I was headed to Leitchfield, the county seat for Grayson. Through my local library, I had found more information, but unless a county has taken the time to scan and/or upload documents to websites, like the one I use, or create books or micro film and distribute those to libraries all over the state… information was limited without travel. So, travel I must.

I had made a recent goal of visiting every county seat in KY. I had only been to eight, but they were all pretty much the same, cute. The courthouse was in the center of a round-a-bout and businesses and little shops were all the way around the opposite side of the street. Leitchfield was no different.

I had located the public library sign (universal for the entire world) as soon as I entered downtown, but I wanted to go to the courthouse first. On Saturdays this courthouse was open until noon and I didn't want to miss the opportunity to get documents that may only be available there. And I had until eight pm to enjoy the library.

I did know by this point that Harrison was Winifred's father and her mother's name was Sarah. I hoped to find a lot about them today. I was a happy camper as I walked into the courthouse, all giggles. As I entered the records room I was immediately greeted.

"How can I help you today?" A very pleasant older lady asked.

"I'm doing genealogy research and I would like to dig around in your marriage records." As always flashing my award-winning smile, puts everyone at ease!

"Oh sure, right though here." She gestured for me to follow her into a smaller room off of the main room. "The copier is over there, someone will count your copies for you at the desk before you leave, and ladder is over there..."

"LADDER!?"

"Yes, I was going to point to the boxes up on the shelf next. You obviously don't have a clue as to what I am talking about." She giggled. "Those boxes are in numeric order according to the marriage certificate numbers. They contain documents relating to the marriages."

"DOCUMENTS!?" Giggling at me again, but she was so cute!

"Of course, every marriage is different, but some of the boxes have permission notes from the parents allowing their children to be married, some have the bond documents showing how much money was obtained to secure the wedding or if the bond was broken, arrest records.... Did you know that is where the term 'shotgun wedding' came from?" I am certain I was looking at her as though she was speaking a foreign language. I was going to burst with excitement.

"No ma'am. I didn't know that. What does that mean exactly?"

"Well, if a girl's father put up $100 for the soon-to-be son-in-law to marry his daughter, and say, the boy got cold feet, lots of times the father would go get him and make him marry her to keep from losing the money, because he had paid the court and they both had signed the bond, and the embarrassment for his daughter. And if the boy got away in the middle of the night, say, then a judge would issue a warrant for his arrest because a bond was a legally binding document. The boy broke the law by breaking his word and 'stealing' the father's money."

"NO WAY!!" *I wondered if she would consider adopting me as like my great Aunt or something.... Lol.*

"If you need anything, dear, just let me know. And be careful with the ladder." *She called me dear! She did want to adopt me! Insert happy dance here. Back to work, silly!!*

Marriage records are typed into books after the fact. So, in early years the bonds were actually bound into the books with the marriage certificate, all in date order. So, she must be talking about early marriage stuff in those boxes. Cool! There are periodic indexes for marriages between this year and this year so that it is easier to find what you're looking for. So, I was looking for a marriage certificate for Winifred Logsdon. She married John Kesinger first and that was in the 1860-ish… so I need……... this book right here. Yeah! And they are in alphabetical order by last name, so she will be in the bride column close to the end of the index. But what about her parents. I did not know her mom's last name. I will look for Harrison first. He had two marriages, both in book #1. Wow! Book #1, that is crazy… Page 6, which was actually the first page of recorded marriages. They were just written in it was so long ago. Guess you could just get married without having to let anyone know like nowadays. I started at the bottom of the page. Up, up, up, I was searching… OH MY GOODNESS! THE 2ND RECORDED MARRIAGE IN GRAYSON COUNTY! Harrison Logsdon to Sarah Saltsman

Chapter 18

The library was about four blocks up Main St. and one right turn. I was so excited about what I had found so far, I was hoping that wasn't the end of my findings for the day. It would be great to find some more fabulous history! I needed the copies of the items I had just found, my tree chart, a small one, and my binder. I think that was it…

Every library has a different way of doing things, I was hoping I could show them my library card and get an internet pass for my visit with them. No need to worry about checking out books, because you can't check out anything from the reference departments, ever! But you can make copies till your heart was content. I walked up to the counter. The chubby little girl with the 50's flip and ratted hairdo and horn-rimmed glasses, gave me the 1 finger because she was on the phone and apparently the only one working the desk. Just a couple minutes and she exploded on me… "Oh my goodness! I have never seen you before! Are you from around here or somewhere else? I see you have some information with you, I hope I can be of help. Isn't it a lovely day? The weather has just been fantastic lately, don't you think? So, what exactly can I do for you today?" I paused…. waiting for her to start talking again. I just looked at her blankly for a second. "No, go ahead. Every-body does that…" she looked down shyly. "apparently I talk a lot." I laughed in spite of myself.

"Well, I was hoping to get an internet pass for the day with my current library card. I have driven about an hour to do some genealogy research here. I would, also, like to access my tree on-line if possible."

"That is fascinating! Where are you from?" She was gen-uinely interested.

"Owensboro."

"Neat-O! Let's have a look at your card and I will give them a call and make sure your current. No fines or anything, right? Never stolen a book, I assume?"

"Oh wow! Never!"

"Ha! Ha! Got you! You don't look dumb enough to walk into a library if you had ever stolen a book!" she nearly gave me a seizure. This one is a wild card I'll have to keep an eye on her. She was off the phone now. "Alrighty, you are good to go! We have one PC in the genealogy room and nobody else is here today, so we will set you up there. Okay?"

"Sure. That sounds great. I have a few questions also, if you have time?"

"Definitely. Let's get this up and going first, and then you can ask while I give you a mini tour." She had the PC humming and on my site in seconds. She motioned for me to walk to my right. "These two cabinets have film; they are indexed on the tag on the front of each drawer. Over there are family files in alphabetical order and on the back side of the bookshelf are the census and cemetery books. Oh, and I almost forgot, under the family files we have school and marriage books, those are new." Well, I thought I was going to have a few questions, but you answered everything for me. You are very helpful, thank you."

"Just come and get me if you need anything. Okay?"

I wanted to get into those Census books, but I really wanted to check and see if I had gotten a response from the woman who had sent me the message through the genealogy web site. I had to type my email and password... 2 messages! Too bad I am not home I would jump for joy.

Tonya, so great to hear from you! I am so glad you thought to explain your relationship to Charles, because we ARE related! How fun is that? Charles was my grandmother's grandfather. I read your profile on the site, so that makes you about the same age as me. I hope you like to share, because I work at the National Archives in Lexington and I have some really awesome stuff on our family. I was hoping you might have some pictures of Charles. My grandmother, Betty, only has one. We should exchange e-mails too, to make it easier to share. Love Elizabeth!

Tears were stinging my eyes I just couldn't believe it. An actual relative… I knew of no family for my dad outside of our huge get togethers. This was absolutely wonderful. But it had said 2! I have another one to read! Woot!!

It has been 2 weeks since I sent the last message. I hope you're doing ok. I told my grandmother about you and she is so excited. She is hoping you have a FB so you can be friends. She has a ton of questions. I hate that I haven't heard from you. I have so much to tell you. Well, I guess I can tell you some of it now. Joe and Charles' brother, Benjamin, derailed a passenger train in Hartford in 1913. I found the newspaper article and I have a copy I want to send you. It is the entire front page of the Hartford Herald, July 30, 1913. And I have a couple other smaller articles from surrounding towns. I hope you are excited now! LOL, your cousin, Elizabeth.

I was pretty sure I was at the brink of overflowing. Like rainbows and skittles were going to start spewing out of me… I couldn't breathe I was so shocked. And I could not wait to share this stuff with my dad's family. First, I had to message her back. She had included her e-mail this time so I would just email her back. And then I wanted to get into those Census books and birth microfilms!

Chapter 19

There was one Census I wanted to see in particular. The 1880 Grayson County census. My library had the 1860 and 1870 and nobody had the 1890 because the Archives that held the original censuses until they were old enough to distribute, had burned and the 1890 was lost forever. With the Soundex version that I had, I wanted to find the Scifers and now the Logsdons in the Census book and see their neighbors. Lots of the time they would be on a family farm with only one residence number, but with several family numbers. So, my fingers were crossed as I looked on the shelf, 60, 70... 80! Yeah! I grabbed the cemetery index also as I walked to the table to sit down.

I opened the book in the very back to find the index. Looking for the 'Sc' names, here we go. I thought. There was one Scifers and two Syphers and a "see also Sifers". The first three were not who I was looking for. See also Sifres, okie dokie. Turn the page, eight Sifres. Cool. Page 8, two on page 27... nope. Page32 & 34... M.J.E. Sifres age 6. WOW! Now, who all is living around them. Powells, Caswells, lots of Alveys. All had initials for their first names. No Logsdons; so back to the index. Only one family of them in the index. Well, I hope that is them and they hadn't moved or died. Winnie's brother was listed as the head of house, but Harrison was living with them. Listed as invalid - I later found out that he died that same year. I should just flip through the back and see if any other sir names could be in Hardin that I have been looking for. Hmmm, there was a Lear. I had recently discovered that Daddy's great times 2 grandmother was Sina (Lear) Duvall. So, I will check, just to be sure. Ugh! There must be 30 pages to check. I almost talked myself out of looking but I had most of the day still, so may as well be sure. A little over halfway through the names, I found a Sina Duvall. Jukey's great-grandmother. But I had found nothing on her. I only had her name because it was on Jukey's grandmother's marriage certificate as her mother and 'I don't know' as the father. I wondered how someone cannot know who their father is. Well, here was Sina and her husband's name was Marion. They had three children, Daddy's great-grandmother, Almarie, being one of them. So cool. I had been looking for more on them and had not found anything. I assumed it was another brick wall. There was something weird though, beside the 'F' for female beside both of their names was a 'M'. Everyone else in the family had a 'W'. I bet there is a glossary somewhere to describe the columns. It was in the front, 'M' meant Mulatto. The hairs were standing up on my neck. I was pretty sure I knew what that meant... but how... my head was spinning. I walked up front to ask 50's girl for a dictionary.

"The oldest one you have here would be great." She obliged me by showing me a shelf full of them. "Take your pick." The oldest one I could find was a 1957 Webster's. "Mulatto: adj. Meaning muddy or dirty in color". Oh wow! I think I just offended myself. Now to Google. "Mulatto is a term used to refer to persons born of one white parent and one black parent, or to persons born of a mulatto parent or parents. The term today is generally confined to a historical context, and English-speakers of mixed white and black ancestry seldom choose to identify themselves as "mulatto". (ref; Google docs.)" The shock I was feeling was overwhelming. I would never have dreamed I would find information like this. I had to get out of here and get some air. I needed to make copies of everything I had here and call my cousin at the Annex in Greenville. I needed her objective ideas.

Twenty minutes later I was in my car. 50's girl nearly talked my leg off while I was paying for my copies and asking if I found anything interesting. *Wowsers, did I.* I had just politely said, nothing major. I wanted to talk to Caro first. I had to plug my phone to the charger. My hands were shaking. Just calm down Tonya, get a grip. Strange voice at the Annex. "Is Caro working today?"

"No." I was going to melt into my seat, I needed her so badly…

"Oh wait! She just walked through the door! Must be your lucky day. Can I ask who is calling?"

"Tonya." Thank you, Jesus!

"Hey cuz. What's up?"

"Well, it's kind of a long story, but I will speed it up." I gave her all the details and explained the Census.

"What do you think?" I was exhausted mentally, but so much better after telling someone.

"I don't even know what to say to you. Are you okay, I mean some people would be devastated? Not that you strike me as that kind of person. I just don't want to offend you."

"No Caro. Just shoot it straight. I need to know what you think."

She let out a long breath. "I would guess that Sina's mother was black, and either she and a white man feel in love, and of course could not marry or Sina was the product of a slave rape by her mother's owner or family member. And if Almarie was also a product of slave rape or her father was white, she would still be listed as Mullato. As for the other children being white, they may be his and not hers. Or they could have been so light that he claimed they were his to get the stigma off of them. Are you okay?" I didn't realize it but I had been holding my breath.

"Yep, I'm good. That was what I was thinking to, all of it. But I wanted an objective opinion. Thanks Caro, I really appreciate your thoughts."

"I hope this doesn't sound ridiculous," she sounded nervous all the sudden, "but, I don't think of you any differently now. Okay?" *Bless her heart!*

"No, it isn't ridiculous. And you read my mind. Thanks, you're a sweetheart!" I love you's and goodbyes and we were off the phone. Guess we connected on a higher level because she had never said I love you before, but we were family so….

I didn't have a problem with the info I got. But, my mom was going to be floored. I hate to admit that my ancestors were racist but it was a different time. My mom grew up in Chicago. We were not southern. I was trying to be an enlightened adult, not live in hatred of others. But Caro was closer to my mom's age than mine, so it was sweet of her to think of saying what she did.

Chapter 20

After about thirty miles of wind blowing through my hair and the dust off my brain. I felt much better. This actually explained a lot. All of daddy's siblings and Felecia having afros and the way we all tan so well and stay pretty much darker than most all year long. And if I had a dollar for every time someone asked me if Felecia was mixed because of her pouty lips and beautiful eyebrows… Just wow! I decided to go to my library when I got into town, just to check if I had gotten a message back from my new cousin. I meant to check before I left Leitchfield, but I wasn't thinking about that.

I pulled into the parking lot about two hours before they would close, so I was good on time. And I wanted to make a big dinner for Felecia tonight and tell her my news. So, I will check my email and head to the house. My sweet old lady friend was working, and she just pointed to number 14 and said you know the password. She is so stinking cute. I just love her to pieces. Oh yea! I did have an email from Elizabeth, and it had attachments. Haha! It was a two-page letter! She was going to be fantastic I could tell already. Four attachments. The first one was the front page of the Hartford Harold that she had promise me. I did eventually get that printed and framed, with Benjamin's picture. The second was the two smaller articles on the train wreck. The third was two photos, Sam Avery and Mary Jane Elizabeth Avery. M. J. E. Scifers! Shut the front door! If she wasn't at least part Indian, I will kiss your big toe. She was dark and had dark eyes and a long neck and straight black hair and high cheek bones. She was lovely. Well even though I know that the head dress in the picture my aunt showed me was not a real one, maybe that's why she took the picture. She knew her heritage, I'm sure. Right? And the fourth was a picture of Charles Avery with her grandmother. Her letter was great. Jumping around to this and that, just full of energy. Telling me more about the articles and the photos. She said the newspaper said that the judge told Benjamin's dad that the "boy was badly spoiled and needed to be taken in hand" and that Benjamin had told the judge "that I was just trying to make a pair of scissors with rail spikes and the first had worked just fine". Oh, my goodness the boy must have been crazy! Then she asked me if I had known that M. J. E. was Indian? What? She said she was at work and didn't have all of her paperwork with her there, but she would send me some documentation on her tribe. Shut up! I just could not believe the day I was having. She said she got her picture from find-a-grave. What is that I wondered. She said I should check into being a contributor. Whatever that meant. I emailed her back and told her about the picture of her in the head dress and that I had pictures of all the Avery boys, including one of Benjamin with a 5-foot catfish he caught out of the Green River. I also told her I had been to Leitchfield that day and what I had on the Scifers and asked if she had as much trouble finding them as I had. Kisses to her and her grandmother and goodbyes.

Now www.findagrave.com. There it is. Now what? Um, *find a memorial. Click.* Coolness. Mary Avery born 1874 died 1917. *Click*, search. Oh, my goodness!! There is the picture Elizabeth just sent me and a copy of her death certificate and a picture of her tombstone. Well, I definitely want to be involved with this whatever it is! Um, go back to home page. Become a contributor, *Click*. Please read our mission statement, *Click*. Short and to the point. We take this site seriously… only get involved if you genuinely want to enrich the lives of other by providing photos of their loved ones… all over the world thousands of photos are uploaded by individuals just like you every day… Select 'yes' if you agree, *Click*. Fill out the form, we will do a brief background check, wow, they are serious, you will know something within 7 to 10 days. Crazy.

Chapter 21

It was a beautiful, crisp autumn day. The sun was shining, and I was going over my upcoming wedding in my head. Several years had passed since I had started this journey and Felecia had grown so much, and so had I really. My life was moving in a positive direction, finally. Brad was my Prince Charming, everything I had thought a man was supposed to be like. I had just imagined that "he" was fictional. That there was no man that was really like that. Except for my stepdad, of course. He was the man to which all men would be measured by, in my life anyway. Two bad divorces and cutting loose of some people that I thought were my friends, had jaded me a little. But I had taken it in stride and came out on the other side, better for it, too. And as my soon to be mother-in-law says, "Some situations cause you to have to grab your big girl panties and trudge on through it! And sometimes what you're trudging through can cause those panties to be pretty darn big!" She was so funny, but she got me and loved me for loving her son. You can't ask for more than that. His entire family was fantastic and had accepted Felecia and my grandbabies as members of the family immediately. His dad told me, "We don't do yours, mine and ours in this family. We are all 'ours'!" I loved them all dearly... *Oh my goodness! Focus, focus, focus!*

I had a membership to the online genealogy website now and had filled in some gaps and made several more trips to visit my dad (in Florida) and his family (in Kentucky), sometimes I got more information and sometimes I got nothing new. But it was great to visit just the same. Today I was driving to Greenville to have lunch with Tammy at our favorite Mexican restaurant. We tried to get together every few months to stay caught up on family and such. I had two failed marriages under my belt, and you know at some point you stop and ask yourself, am I the problem here? But I knew deep down that I had not caused them to cheat, they just made that choice for themselves.

About eight months ago, with my dad dying and my second marriage falling apart, I decided it was time to get back to what I needed and that was to finish this journey. Jax had called me and said he had given up, Dad had decided not to do dialysis anymore, and he was just too tired to fight. I had just started a new job and they agreed to give me some time off, but just one occasion, not two. I made up my mind to go see him while he was alive, I still had questions I had not been brave enough ask just yet. So, I packed my big girl panties, and I would ask the hard questions first, so I could apologize afterwards if necessary.

I rented a car and drove to Florida. My sister was at Jax's waiting for me. She was three months pregnant with my nephew and had a little bitty baby bump. Oh, how I loved that bump already. Amy and I had gotten closer with the recent visits I had made specifically for that reason. I only had two days to make this visit count. So, when Amy asked what I wanted to do first, I said I need to see him. So, off we went. He was receiving hospice care at a nursing home just a couple miles up the road. He was in really bad shape, we had to put on scrubs and gloves and masks, to keep from transferring germs. All he could see was our eyes and he knew us both immediately. "There's my girls right there!" he said to his nurse as we came through the door. "Hi Daddy!" I rushed to him to kiss his forehead, from behind my mask. "I didn't know you were coming, Sug."

"I wanted to talk to you before you were gone." I had taken one of Jax's Xanax so I could get through this without having a meltdown.

"Do you want me to go?"

"No, I want you to stay." I smiled at her, from behind my mask. She smiled back because her eyes squinted.

"Could you rub your hands up and down my legs, the fluid

is making my skin itch." Daddy asked.

"Keep your gloves on and no scratching." The nurse said as she was leaving. "Call me with the button if you need anything."

"I'm so glad you're here," he said.

"Daddy I want to ask you about Scott." My voice was trembling. Amy jerked her head toward me. But I couldn't read her face behind the mask. He just closed his eyes and took a breath.

"I knew this day would come sooner or later. I had thought I may get off this earth without having to tell you. Are you mad?"

"I have tried very hard not to be. But sometimes I fail. I am not mad right now. Just curious. And it doesn't matter how I found out. I just need to know. Does he know about me? Does he want to meet me? What does he look like?"

"Amy, will you tell Jackie to give Tonya all the pictures of him when you get back to the house?" She was patting his forehead and nodding her head. *Whoa! Whoa! Whoa! Amy knew him?* He turned his head to look at me. "Your mom made me promise never to tell you. She didn't want you to feel like you weren't special to me, because I had another child. After we divorced and I married Jackie, I tried to tell her you weren't jealous of Amy and you loved her, and I thought you would take it okay. She was afraid by that time you would be angry because we had never told you. So, we just left it. be."

"You were married to his mom?"

"Yes, but not when she got pregnant. I was married to your mother and he is just a few months older than you. I am so sorry, Sug. I am sure that is the real reason she didn't want you to know. Because I cheated on her." I was wishing I had another Xanax. "Your mother is a great woman. And I never treated her right. I know now I will answer for what I have done. I know I was never a good father to you, but you have had Walter and I tried to be a good dad to Amy. I hope that can make up for it a little." She was crying and patting him. In that single moment, it did make up for it. She loved him, he had walked her down the aisle, he had raised her and spanked her when she needed it. Fudd had gotten my cars worked on, gave me money for deposits on apartments, and loved Felecia like his own grandchild. All the things you do for your grown children. That's why I had never been mad at Daddy before, it had not made much difference.

"I'm not mad at you Daddy. And you have been a great father to Amy and for that I am very grateful. You did a great job with her. She is smart and beautiful and kind. You can't ask for anything more."

"I love you both. You know that right?" We both said I love you to at the same time which made him laugh. We stayed and helped him with his lunch and then he was tired, so we left with the promise of coming back later.

We visited him three more times before I had to go home. It was hard to leave, knowing I would never see he him again. But I never regretted my decision to see him instead of going to the funeral, we both, well I guess all three of us had needed it. Jax had given me all of Daddy's pictures. Instead of just the ones of Scott. Most of them were of me and mom or Felecia anyway. He had pictures of himself with Scott when he was just a little boy, where had I been. And some of Scott and Amy in their house in Richland. I had been out of the loop for sure.

I had been home two days and my BFF, MiShawn, and I were buying each other mani/pedis for Mother's day, which was the next day. Felecia was going to meet us there. She was picking up her cap and gown from the school for graduation and was going to bring it to the salon to show us her senior key and all that stuff. When MiShawn pulled up beside me in the parking lot of the salon, I was on the phone. She waved and jumped out of her car and into the passenger of mine. She was looking at me with concern. Her 'what is it' face. "Okay. I love you too. Bye."

"What? What happened?"

"That was Jax. Daddy's gone. He was in a lot of pain through the night, and they gave him morphine and just kept upping it until it took him. Which I am told that is basically what they do. Just make them comfortable until the Lord takes them home." She was holding my hand,

"Are you all right, honey?"

"I'm a little in shock, I think. But I knew it was coming. I'm glad he isn't suffering anymore. And he accepted Christ while I was there, so I know I will see him again."

"Do you still want to go inside? I will understand if you don't want to do this today."

"No, I'm good. We made our peace and he's looking down on me now. Gotta keep on keepin' on."

About a year later I was the kitchen manager of a local restaurant and I saw someone I thought I knew come in and I went out front to check. It was one of the boys that grew up with my Avery cousins. He had lived right across the road from Tammy. I had actually thought he was my cousin for a long time. He saw me and got up to give me a hug. We chatted briefly and then I had to get back in the kitchen. He asked if I work every day and I said yep except for weekends and Mondays I left at 11 instead of 1. About two weeks later I saw him come in with two guys, one I recognized as his brother the other looked familiar, but I couldn't place him. I walked out front to hug my non-cousin and he saw me and motioned to the other guy who stood up to greet me. As I got closer, I realized why he looked familiar. "Hi." He was holding out his hand to shake mine. "I'm your brother, Scott." He looked just like Daddy...